THE ROSE CODEX

A Rose Pocket Sanctuary Series™ - Volume I

The Rose Codex
A Rose Pocket Sanctuary Series™ - Volume I

This Pocket Sanctuary is intended for personal spiritual enrichment and reflection. It is not meant to replace professional, medical, or therapeutic guidance.

Published by Rooted Hound Press
Vienna, New Jersey
rootedhoundpress.com

Cover design by Rooted Hound Press.

ISBN 978-1-969687-07-5

Printed in the United States of America.

First Edition: 2025

The Rose Series™ – Pocket Sanctuaries

A devotional collection exploring the Rose Lineage, the feminine path of remembrance, and the quiet wisdom that awakens the soul.

Volume I
The Rose Codex
A guide to the ancient symbolism of the Rose and the heart-centered path of awakening.

Volume II
Mary Magdalene: A Sanctuary of Remembrance
A restoration of the Magdalene's voice, presence, and feminine wisdom.

Volume III

The Magdalene Path
An embodied guide to living the Rose teachings through daily devotion, truth, softness, and inner remembrance.

Forthcoming Volumes
The Magdalene Path: Daily Practices
The Lost Feminine Gospels
The Rose Priestess
The Rose at the End of the World
(Additional volumes will continue to unfold.)

To every soul who has ever felt the quiet pull of their own heart. May this rose remind you that you are unfolding exactly as you were meant to.

*Before words,
before stories, before you learned who you were expected to be—
there was a heartbeat inside you
that already knew the way home.
The Rose remembers this.
And through her,
you remember too.*

Contents

Introduction—"The Rose as a Teacher"

There are symbols humanity has carried for thousands of years—symbols that appear across cultures, religions, and spiritual traditions, all speaking in their own way about the same truth.

The **rose** is one of them.

For Christians, the rose has long been associated with the sacred heart, divine compassion, and the quiet strength of Mary and Mary Magdalene. For mystics, it represents remembrance—returning to the wisdom already seeded within the soul. For spiritual seekers, it is a map of self-discovery, unfolding one petal at a time. For intuitive and earth-based practitioners, its spiral core reflects nature's oldest teaching: that all growth is cyclical, layered, and ever-deepening.

In every tradition, the rose is not simply a flower. It is a **teacher.**

She shows us:

- how to open without rushing
- how to hold softness and strength together
- how to protect what is sacred while still blooming
- how to grow at the pace of truth
- how to return to ourselves again and again

The teachings in this Pocket Sanctuary are not new. They are ancient. They live in stories, scripture, mysticism, and nature itself. But the Rose offers them in a way we can feel, not just understand.

This is why I call it **The Rose Codex**—a collection of teachings written not on pages, but in petals, thorns, fragrance, and spiral.

This Pocket Sanctuary is an invitation to explore the wisdom the Rose has carried for centuries: the wisdom of the heart, the wisdom of the soul, and the wisdom of remembrance.

HOW TO USE THIS SANCTUARY

This Pocket Sanctuary is meant to be read slowly.

You do not need to complete it in one sitting. You do not need to take notes or "keep up." You do not need any prior knowledge of the Rose, Mary Magdalene, or spiritual symbolism.

Simply move at the pace that feels natural to you.

Each section offers:

✦ A Teaching

A gentle explanation of the Rose's wisdom and how it applies to your everyday life.

✦ An Affirmation

A sentence to anchor the lesson into your heart.

✦ A Journaling Prompt

A doorway for deeper inner exploration.

There is no right way to use this Sanctuary. You may:

      read one section a day

      move intuitively between pages

      return to certain teachings when needed

      use this as part of a morning ritual

      keep it by your bedside

read it quietly with tea

tuck it into your bag as a reminder of your path

Let this Sanctuary be what it was designed to be:

A small companion. A gentle teacher. A reminder that your soul unfolds one petal at a time.

When you're ready, turn the page and enter the first teaching.

SECTION 1 — WHAT IS THE ROSE CODEX

The First Petal
Before the teachings,
before the symbols,
before the stories we try to make sense of—
there is only a quiet opening.
A single petal turning toward the light,
whispering a truth you have always known:
you were made to return to yourself.

The Rose Codex is an ancient way of understanding the inner life of the soul, expressed through the simple but powerful symbolism of the rose. Across cultures and traditions, the rose has been used to represent love, compassion, truth, devotion, and the unfolding of the spiritual journey. In Christian tradition, it is closely connected to Mary and Mary Magdalene, whose lives reflect courage, devotion, and the quiet strength of a heart aligned with the divine. In mystical circles, the rose is a symbol of remembrance—the idea that spiritual awakening is not something new we acquire, but something we return to within ourselves. And in natural wisdom traditions, the rose is a living teacher whose petals, fragrance, and thorns communicate lessons about growth, protection, softness, timing, and sacred boundaries.

The Codex itself is not a written text or a single historical document. It is a way of seeing. It is the understanding that the rose teaches through form, rhythm, and pattern. The way it opens slowly teaches patience and timing. The presence of both bloom and thorn teaches polarity and balance. The fragrance teaches resonance and the unseen impact of our energy. The spiral at the heart of the rose teaches that life is cyclical and that lessons return so we can meet them with new understanding.

In this Pocket Sanctuary, the Rose Codex is presented as a collection of teachings anyone can access—regardless of religious background or spiritual path. It does not require belief in any specific doctrine. It simply invites you to notice what the rose has always been teaching: that your heart has a way of knowing, your soul has a natural rhythm, and your unfolding is sacred.

Affirmation:

I honor the wisdom alive within me, and I open to it one petal at a time.

Journaling Prompt:

What part of yourself feels like it is beginning to open, or open again? What inner truth feels familiar, as if you are remembering rather than learning it for the first time?

SECTION 2 — WHY THE ROSE MATTERS

Why We Are Drawn
We lean toward the rose
not because it blooms,
but because something in us
recognizes the way it opens.
Softly.
Patiently.
In truth,
and in time.

We are drawn to the rose for reasons that go far beyond its beauty. Something in us recognizes it. The rose mirrors the inner life of the soul in a way few symbols can. It shows us how growth happens—not by force, but by invitation. It reminds us that strength and softness are not opposites but companions. And it teaches that our true unfolding happens when we are rooted, nurtured, and aligned with the light that calls us forward.

The rose matters because it speaks in a language the heart understands. When we observe how a rose opens, we witness the natural rhythm of awakening. When we see its thorns, we remember the necessity of boundaries that protect what is sacred. When we breathe in its fragrance, we are reminded that our presence has an unseen impact on those around us. Every part of the rose carries wisdom that reflects the journey of becoming who we truly are.

Spiritually, the rose has held significance for centuries. It has been a symbol of the sacred heart, the divine feminine, devotion, healing, and the quiet power of love expressed through truth. In many traditions, the rose is seen as a living representation of divine compassion—the kind of love that does not bypass struggle, but transforms it. This is why the rose is considered a teacher. Through its form and its nature, it mirrors the deeper truths of the human spirit.

The rose matters because it helps us remember what we often forget: that our unfolding is not something to rush, control, or perfect. It is something to honor.

Affirmation:

My growth is sacred, and I honor the rhythm of my unfolding.

Journaling Prompt:

What part of your life is asking to be approached with softness instead of force? Where might you be trying to bloom before you feel ready?

SECTION 3 — THE THORN & BLOOM PRINCIPLE

The Dual Wisdom

You were never meant
to bloom without protection,
nor guard yourself so tightly
that nothing living could reach you.
The rose shows the way—
soft petal, sharp thorn,
each made holy by the other.

Every rose carries both bloom and thorn. One draws us in; the other protects what is precious. Together, they reveal a truth at the heart of spiritual growth: our softness and our strength are not opposites. They belong to one another.

The bloom represents openness, compassion, vulnerability, beauty, tenderness, and the willingness to be seen. It is the part of us that reaches toward connection and expresses our inner truth. The thorn represents boundaries, discernment, self-respect, honesty, and the ability to stand firm. It is the part of us that protects what is sacred within.

Many of us have been taught to choose one or the other— to be only gentle, or only guarded. But the rose shows us that both are needed. A bloom without a thorn cannot protect itself. A thorn without a bloom has nothing to protect. When we deny our softness, we lose the ability to connect. When we deny our strength, we lose the ability to stay safe.

The Thorn & Bloom Principle teaches that balance is essential. It invites us to soften where we have hardened too much, and strengthen where we have been too open too soon. It reminds us that compassion does not mean allowing harm, and boundaries do not mean withdrawing from love. True maturity lives in the union of both.

This principle is deeply reflected in the spiritual stories connected to the rose. Mary Magdalene, often associated with the rose lineage, embodied compassion without losing her clarity. She offered presence, devotion, and truth—yet she remained unwavering in her sense of self. This is the teaching of the rose: you can be open without being unprotected, and strong without being closed.

When we live with both thorn and bloom, we honor the fullness of who we are. We allow ourselves to open while safeguarding our heart. We learn to say yes from authenticity and no from self-respect. And we become rooted, resilient, and able to grow in alignment with truth.

Affirmation:

My softness is sacred, and my strength is sacred. Both protect and express who I am.

Journaling Prompt:

Where in your life are you being called to soften? Where are you being called to strengthen a boundary or stand more firmly in truth?

SECTION 4 — HOW TO LIVE BY THE ROSE CODE

The Way of the Rose
She never hurries,
never forces,
never pretends to be open
before she feels the warmth to do so.
Yet she trusts herself enough
to bloom when the moment is true.

The Rose Code is not a doctrine or a strict set of rules. It is a way of living—a gentle, heart-centered rhythm that guides how we relate to ourselves, to others, and to the world around us. The Rose teaches through her nature, and when we observe her closely, we find a pattern for living with wisdom, compassion, and integrity.

To live by the Rose Code is to honor timing. A rose does not rush to open; it blooms when conditions are right. In our own lives, this means recognizing that growth cannot be forced. We are allowed to move slowly, to take time, and to unfold at a pace that feels true. This is not avoidance—it is alignment.

To live by the Rose Code is to value both softness and strength. Just as the rose holds petals and thorns, we hold compassion and boundaries. Living the Rose Code means practicing kindness without abandoning self-respect, offering love without losing ourselves, and knowing that both gentleness and firmness can be expressions of truth.

To live by the Rose Code is to cultivate inner resonance. A rose's fragrance extends beyond what the eye can see; its presence affects the environment around it. Our energy works the same way. When we act from authenticity, speak from clarity, and lead with sincerity, we leave an imprint that reaches farther than our words. The Rose Code invites us to become intentional about the energy we carry into our relationships, work, and daily life.

To live by the Rose Code is to return—again and again—to the heart. The rose teaches remembrance. In moments of confusion, we are called back to what is simple, true, and deeply known within us. We return to compassion, honesty, and quiet devotion. We return to the inner guidance that gently rises when we are still enough to listen.

Living this way does not require perfection. It requires presence. It means choosing truth over performance, intention over impulse, and love over fear. It means showing up as we are, while continuing to unfold into who we are becoming.

The Rose Code is, at its center, an invitation: Live with depth. Live with discernment. Live with an open and protected heart. Live in a way that honors your own sacred unfolding.

Affirmation:

I honor my natural rhythm and choose to live with intention, compassion, and truth.

Journaling Prompt:

What is one way you can live more intentionally this week—
either through timing, boundaries, compassion, or the energy
you bring into a space?

SECTION 5 — THE SPIRAL OF THE ROSE

The Center

At the heart of every turning,
there is a deeper place within you
waiting to be met.
What looks like returning
is really the next circle in your becoming.

At the very center of every rose is a spiral—a quiet, elegant pattern that appears not only in flowers, but throughout nature, art, architecture, and even the growth of galaxies. The spiral is one of the oldest symbols of spiritual growth, and its presence within the rose reveals an essential truth: awakening is not linear. It unfolds in cycles.

To understand the spiral is to understand that life moves through seasons of returning. We revisit lessons, emotions, relationships, and inner thresholds not because we have failed, but because we are meeting them from a deeper place within ourselves. This repeating is not failure; it is how the soul expands.

The spiral teaches that every return brings new wisdom. Each time we circle back, we carry more understanding, more compassion, more clarity, and more truth. What once felt confusing begins to feel purposeful. What once felt overwhelming begins to reveal meaning. What once felt like starting over becomes a continuation of who we are becoming.

The Rose mirrors this beautifully. Her petals do not open in a straight line—they unfold in soft, spiraling layers. This is how our own inner unfolding happens: gently, gradually, and with repeated openings that lead us closer to the heart of who we are.

For many, the spiral is also a symbol of divine timing. It reminds us that growth cannot be rushed and that each stage of our journey prepares us for the next. Even when it feels like we are circling back to old patterns or emotions, we are not in the same place we were before. We have widened. We have deepened. We have grown.

If you feel called to explore the symbolism of the spiral more fully, I offer a deeper companion piece in my book *Echoes Through the Spiral: A Soul's Continuum.* It expands on this wisdom through the lens of remembrance, cycles, and the geometry of the soul. But for the purpose of this Sanctuary, it is enough to simply recognize: the spiral is the natural shape of your becoming.

Your life is not meant to be a straight line. It is meant to be an unfolding.

Affirmation:

Every time I return, I rise. My growth is a spiral, and I honor its wisdom.

Journaling Prompt:

What is one lesson, emotion, or pattern you've revisited recently? How does it feel different now than the last time you experienced it?

SECTION 6 — THE ROSE RITUAL

The Unfolding
You do not open all at once.
You open in breaths,
in moments,
in tiny softenings
that only the heart can measure.

This simple ritual is designed to help you connect with the heart of the Rose Codex. It requires no specific belief system, no sacred tools, and no elaborate preparation. It is a moment of quiet alignment—a way to return to yourself with intention.

Begin by finding a comfortable place to sit. You may hold a rose, a petal, a sachet, or nothing at all. The ritual works with whatever you have, because the essence of it lives within you.

Close your eyes and take a slow breath in through your nose, allowing your chest to lift gently. As you exhale, let your shoulders soften. With your next inhale, imagine that you are breathing into the center of your chest—the inner space the Rose symbolizes. Feel the area behind your breastbone expand as if a small light were being tended there.

Now bring to mind something in your life that feels tender, sacred, or in need of gentle attention. This might be a longing, a fear, a truth you are learning to speak, or a part of yourself that is trying to open. Hold it gently in your awareness, as you might hold a delicate bloom.

Place your hand over your heart. In your own words or in silence, acknowledge this part of you with compassion. You do not need to fix anything. You do not need to force anything to change. Simply honor what is present.

Then, take one more slow breath and imagine that your heart is opening one petal at a time. Not rushed. Not forced. Just a natural, quiet unfolding. With each breath, allow a little more space, a little more light, a little more truth to arise.

When you feel ready, whisper—either aloud or inwardly: **"May I open at the pace of truth. May I honor what is sacred within me."**

Sit with this for a moment. Let the energy settle. When you are ready, slowly open your eyes.

This ritual can be repeated anytime you feel unsteady, overwhelmed, or disconnected. It is a way of returning to yourself—a miniature pilgrimage back to your own heart, guided by the wisdom of the Rose.

Affirmation:

I open gently, trustingly, and only at the pace that feels true to my heart.

Journaling Prompt:

After practicing the ritual, what shifted inside you? Did anything soften, clarify, or rise to the surface?

THE THREE MYSTERIES OF THE ROSE

A deeper unfolding of the Codex—where what is hidden is gently revealed.

THE FIRST MYSTERY — THE HIDDEN LIFE

Beneath every blossom lies a quiet world unseen.
Where roots drink in the dark, the soul learns to trust what grows
without witness.

There is a part of your journey that no one else will ever see. This hidden life is not empty or forgotten—it is the secret chamber of your becoming. Just as the rose gathers strength underground before it dares to surface, your spirit gathers wisdom in places no one applauds, affirms, or notices. The Hidden Life teaches that the most sacred growth often happens in silence, where your roots learn who they truly are. You are allowed to grow quietly. You are allowed to hold things close. You are allowed to let what is unseen strengthen you before the world ever sees the bloom.

Affirmation

My unseen growth is holy, and it strengthens everything I am becoming.

Journaling Prompt

What is quietly growing within you right now—something not yet visible, but deeply alive beneath the surface?

THE SECOND MYSTERY — THE UNFOLDING

No rose opens all at once.
Every petal waits for its moment.
Unfolding is the art of divine timing.

The rose never forces itself open; it softens with the light, breathes with the morning, and trusts the rhythm written within it. The Unfolding reminds you that your path will open in stages, and each stage is perfect. There is no lateness in the language of the soul. There is only the gentle sequence of becoming—one layer at a time. When you soften your grip on timelines, comparisons, and expectations, your life begins to open exactly as it was always meant to. You are allowed to take your time. You are allowed to open slowly.

Affirmation

I unfold in my own sacred rhythm, guided by a wisdom older than fear.

Journaling Prompt

Where in your life are you feeling pressured to "bloom faster," and how can you instead allow a softer unfolding?

THE THIRD MYSTERY — THE FRAGRANCE

Every rose carries a scent that tells a truth older than words.
The soul has its own fragrance—what lingers after we soften into who
we truly are.

Fragrance is the essence the rose gives freely once it has opened. It is the memory of sunlight, rain, and every silent hour of becoming. In the same way, your life carries a fragrance—made of your compassion, your presence, your kindness, your resilience, your truth. The Mystery of the Fragrance teaches that what you offer the world cannot be forced or fabricated. It emerges naturally when you live aligned with your deeper self. When you stop trying to be anything other than what you are, your true scent rises. It reaches those who are meant to find you.

Affirmation

My presence carries a quiet truth that blesses the spaces I enter.

Journaling Prompt

What qualities, when you live them fully, feel like the "fragrance" your soul naturally offers the world?

THE THORNS — SACRED BOUNDARIES

Even the gentlest rose protects itself.
A thorn is not a weapon—it is a boundary that guards the sacred.

Thorns remind us that softness and strength are not opposites—they belong together. A rose does not apologize for its thorns; it simply stands in the truth that what is precious deserves protection. In your own life, boundaries are the thorns that keep your spirit from being trampled or drained. They are the quiet lines that honor your worth, your time, and your energy. Setting a boundary is not an act of rejection—it is an act of devotion to what allows you to remain open and blooming. You can be gentle and still say no. You can be kind and still keep yourself safe.

Affirmation

My boundaries honor my worth and protect what is sacred within me.

Journaling Prompt

Where in your life is a new boundary needed so your heart can stay open without being depleted?

SYMBOL KEY — THE LANGUAGE OF THE ROSE

The Rose

The unfolding soul. A symbol of spiritual remembrance, awakening, and divine feminine wisdom.

The Stem

The path that carries you—your lived journey, your strength, your endurance.

The Roots

Your origin, ancestry, grounding, and unseen foundations. Where your hidden life gathers strength.

The Thorns

Sacred boundaries. Discernment. Protection of what is precious and true.

The Light

Revelation, clarity, divine guidance—the moments when the next step becomes clear.

The Dew

Grace. The small blessings that appear without explanation, nourishing you in quiet ways.

The Garden

The environment in which you grow—your relationships, choices, practices, and inner landscape.

The Fragrance

Your presence, essence, truth, and the subtle offerings you bring into the world simply by being aligned.

CLOSING BLESSING — "The Heart That Remembers"

May your heart return to itself with kindness. May you honor the pace of your unfolding. May you hold your softness as sacred, and your strength as a gift.

May you trust the seasons of your life, the spirals that deepen your wisdom, and the quiet openings that guide you home.

May the rose remind you that every part of your journey—every petal, every thorn, every return, every rising—has been leading you toward truth.

And may you walk forward from here rooted, steady, and gently blooming into who you were always meant to be.

PUBLICATIONS BY ROOTED HOUND PRESS

The Rose Series™ — Pocket Sanctuaries
The Rose Codex
Mary Magdalene: A Sanctuary of Remembrance
The Magdalene Path
(Additional titles forthcoming)

Pocket Sanctuary Series™
Whispers from the Soul
The Test That I Refused
(Future mini-sanctuaries coming soon)

Books by Rooted Hound Press

Returning to Wholeness: An Invitation to the Soul
Echoes Through the Spiral: A Soul's Continuum
Healing the Past Through the Present
Encoded in Stone: The Memory of Earth & The Story of Us
Thoth & the Tablets: A Journey Through the Crystalline Codes
The Adventures of Layla and Lilly (Children's Series)

Journals & Companions
Rooted Reflections Journal
The Rose Journal
Celestial Journal
Floral Journal
(Additional themed journals coming soon)

Published by
Rooted Hound Press
Vienna, New Jersey
www.rootedhoundpress.com

www.ingramcontent.com/pod-product-compliance
Lightning Source LLC
Chambersburg PA
CBHW071941020426
42331CB00010B/2967